ELECTRICITY COMES TO COCOA BOTTOM

ELECTRICITY COMES TO COCOA BOTTOM

MARCIA DOUGLAS

P E E P A L   T R E E

First published in Great Britain in 1999
Reprinted 2003
Peepal Tree Press Ltd
17 King's Avenue
Leeds LS6 1QS

ISBN 1 900715 28 7

For my parents

and in memory and imagination
of our ancestors

ACKNOWLEDGEMENTS

Some of the poems in *Electricity Comes to Cocoa Bottom*
have previously appeared in *Tar River Poetry*, Volume 35, Number 2;
Sun Dog: The Southeast Review, Volume 15, Number 1;
Phoebe: Journal of Feminist Scholarship Theory and Aesthetics, Volume 8,
Number 1 & 2; *Ma Comère: Journal of the Association of Caribbean Women
Writers and Scholars*, Volume 1, 1998; *Concourse* 8
and *Sisters of Caliban: Contemporary Women Poets of the Caribbean*,
Azul Editions: Falls Church, VA, 1996.

Special thanks to all the family members, colleagues and teachers
who have encouraged and supported this project.

To know birth and to know death
In one emotion
To look before and after
With one eye
To see the Whole
To know the Truth
To know the world
And be without a world;

In this light that is no light;
This time that is no time
To be
And to be free...
>   – BASIL McFARLANE

So whenever you see the Nancy-like filament in the light bulb take care of it. It can light you to the morning. Brer Nancy in a kumbla but he still has power to show you the way
>   –ERNA BRODBER, *Jane and Louisa Will Soon Come Home*

CONTENTS

FIREFLY

ELECTRICITY COMES TO COCOA BOTTOM

Then all the children of Cocoa Bottom
went to see Mr. Samuel's electric lights.
They camped on the grass bank outside his house,
their lamps filled with oil,
waiting for sunset,
watching the sky turn yellow, orange.
Grannie Patterson across the road
peeped through the crack in her porch door.
The cable was drawn like a pencil line across the sun.
The fireflies waited in the shadows,
their lanterns off.
The kling-klings swooped in from the hills,
congregating in the orange trees.
A breeze coming home from sea held its breath;
bamboo lining the dirt road stopped its swaying,
and evening came as soft as chiffon curtains:
Closing. Closing.

Light!
Mr. Samuel smiling on the verandah –
a silhouette against the yellow shimmer behind him –
and there arising such a gasp,
such a fluttering of wings,
tweet-a-whit,
such a swaying, swaying.
Light! Marvellous light!
And then the breeze rose up from above the trees,
swelling and swelling into a wind
such that the long grass bent forward
stretching across the bank like so many bowed heads.
And a voice in the wind whispered:
Is there one among us to record this moment?
But there was none –

no one (except for a few warm rocks
hidden among mongoose ferns) even heard a sound.
Already the children of Cocoa Bottom
had lit their lamps for the dark journey home,
and it was too late —
the moment had passed.

ON YOUR WEDDING DAY

you soak in an enamel basin
and lather your skin with pink soap.
The water is warm,
drawn from the Rio Bueno,
heated on your mother's wood stove.
Crushed aloe floats on top.
Spread for you on the bed
is the towel you were wrapped in at birth.
It smells of khus khus root
and old cardboard boxes;
you wrap yourself in its warmth,
the whites of your eyes shine.
For weeks you have massaged your knees with cocoa butter,
the red soil is gone from your toenails,
lace underwear covers hairs
coiled and glistening,
your dress swirls around your waist
like an upside down hibiscus –
it has cost you two harvests of bananas
and a year of sewing by kerosene light.
One by one you have stitched on the white beads
saved from a broken necklace,
and a satin ribbon borrowed from one of your mother's dresses.
The white shoes you wear
were bought new from town,
the inside soles have the words "Princess Eva"
in golden letters.
Now you pin bougainvillea in your hair
smooth your eyebrows with rosewater
and pat your lips with coconut oil.
A hazy film has covered the yard;
someone has spread petals on the porch steps.
You walk under an archway of palm fronds,
across a carpet of ferns,

your eyelids lowered,
fringed shadows under your eyes.
You feel him standing there
dark and poreless.
You see the tips of his fingers,
the skin of his palms.
Tonight, he will hold you
like the last
spoonful of wine in the world.
Tomorrow you will run barefoot to the river,
red soil in your toenails,
laughing.

COMING BACK

So my Uncle Isaac's baby's one-foot
mother, Myrtle, turns up on his doorstep
after she been missing six long months now,
and he done drink a rum bottle full of
living eye-water from baby bawling
like a forced ripe mango, small and yellow.
Now she hanging white diapers in surrender
tip-toe on her one-foot in the backyard,
dry breasts hidden under her one good frock,
he holding his belly big and pregnant,
six strands of hair like guinea grass on his head.

MURLINE

Me and my best friend Murline
play dandy-shandy at Marse Lloyd's store front.
We sit on the steps.
Her hands clap over mine,
the prints on our palms match –
five, ten.
We clap our knees, clap five.
Clap our knees, clap five.
Clap our knees, clap ten. Clap ten.
Cut off
Nanny tail.
Hang
Nanny tail
from the
man-
go
tree.

Me and my best friend Murline.
The pot holes in the road deepen,
and I go to college.
She stays at Marse Lloyd's store front
selling peeled oranges, tamarind and jew plums soaked in salt water.
The men at the rum shop across the street
watch her body from the corners of their eyes.
From miles away I hear her voice
high and sweet like ripe bombay:
Cut off
Nanny tail.
Hang
Nanny tail
from the man-
go
tree.

Holidays, I come home searching the streets for childhood songs.
Murline round and puffy as a spoiled potato, remembers.
Remembers.
Holding up my hands before her,
the palms dark and criss-crossed like dirt tracks,
we clap our knees. Clap ten.
Clap our hands. Clap ten.
Clap ten. Ten. Ten. Ten. Ten.
Cut off
Nanny tail.
Hang
Nanny tail
from the
man-
go tree.

Now a baby sucks the hem of Murline's skirt.
She has rotting teeth and a missing finger
Her oranges turn soft in the hot sun.
A white film over her eyes,
the school children drop pennies in her basket,
their songs pure as fresh milk:
Cut off
Nanny tail.
Hang
Nanny tail
from the
man-
go
tree.

VIOLA LEE

A patchwork of dry leaves –
nobody's as old as Viola Lee.
I breathe softly in her presence,
touch her only with my fingertips,
shut the door against the wind,
listen for her voice –
a brush against the zinc roof.

When dengue fever broke out
she soaked her braids in bay rum,
wrapped her head with banana leaves and
a cotton scarf bought at May Pen market.
Now she has a bay rum smell,
her forehead a fossil pressed with banana leaf lines.
In her bosom under a withered breast
is a guava leaf from when she and Floyd,
succulent and ripe,
courted under the trees at Thomas River
and he tickled her there.
A small periwinkle leaf,
from the bush that grows over her mother's grave,
covers her navel like a lid.
The periwinkles, Viola Lee says,
hold the secret to where her navel string is buried.
Their lavender heads nod in her dreams –
reaffirming her belief.
Viola Lee's lips are lined with squares of ginger root leaf.
She found these growing by the side of the house
after Floyd ran of to Annotto Bay
with the duppy fly-trap woman, Erma.
(Viola Lee always did say that ginger was
good for getting rid of a bad taste in the mouth.)
Mrs. Kirkpatrick, who studied palm reading abroad,
traced the lines in Viola Lee's hands,

prophesied that she will be dead within a month.
What Mrs. Kirkpatrick doesn't know
is that the veins in those palms
are seams of dead evergreens from Viola Lee's own backyard.
Nobody's as old as Viola Lee.

Now Viola sits on the edge of her bed,
dog-eared as an old almanac.
I close the door behind me,
soft, so as not to disturb her,
leave flowers on the table —
orchids,
pink and young.

LULLABY

Christmas breeze   rocks the crocus-bag awning,
      and the boy selling ginger lilies sucks his thumb,
   tapping his foot to calypso carols on the rum shop radio.
He watches his mother across the street;
      she balances a bucket of anthuriums on her head,
yellow roses in her arms,

held like the yellow baby with thin arms
she once rocked and rocked beneath the awning,
counting its yellow fingers and toes, stroking its head
      while the boy counted change and sucked his thumb,
and the card players danced in the street
              to *Mary's Boy Child* blasting the radio

          the radio the radio. *"Waant a virgin!"* the DJ radio
man shouted, and children waved balloons from their arms,
      blowing fee-fees, skipping rope in the street
as the mother watched the sky through the hole in the awning,
and the boy changed over to the other thumb,
   dancers snapping fingers, bobbing their heads,

          swaying like the lily heads
rejoicing for the boy child on the radio.
Soon, yu goin be too big fe dat t'umb,
his mother had grumbled, and the boy felt old, leaning against her arm,
watching the baby's eyes fixed on the hole in the awning,
undisturbed by the merry makers in the street.

Christmas, and he watches his mother walk the streets,
 the anthuriums in her bucket, grooved like the furrow in her forehead.
      Mi yellow baby him dead and gone, inna de blue hole in the awning,
she cried. And he pictures the pretty boy child on the radio,
playing with the yellow baby, yellow roses in their arms,
and blowing fee-fees and sucking their thumbs,

listening to the children's voices in the street,
closing their eyes, leaning against the wall sturdy as his mother's arms,
long time ago in Bethlehem, on the radio,
rain dropping, dropping through the hole in the awning,

onto the ginger lilies,
his mother's anthuriums across the street.

A THIN SWIFT LIGHT

For hours the shadows move
    in and out
of the hospital room,
pausing by the doorway,
    hovering above,
blocking your view.

The ceiling – wide and smooth like fresh calico – calms you,
and you stitch on it all day
requilting your Eight-Pointed Star –
the one you pieced from bright scraps (saffron and amber),
for eighty years
and eight children.
Now the shadows surround your bed,
hushed and still like the moment between each Word of God.
This has been a long project –
you've liked your stitches small and straight.
Your fingers shaky
you take your time,
thread in thread out

      stitch   by stitch   by stitch   by
      stitch   by stitch   by stitch   by
      stitch   by–

You must rise up on your elbow
holler for one of the children
to come in from the yard and thread your needle
with
strong
black
thread
strong
black
thread

24

for
the eye—)

Tonight,
only you see the needle disappear from the calico —
a thin swift light like a falling star

KING STREET

Deaf Maggie weaves
in and out of the crowd,
holding out a cup for loose change;
she picks at the cup's styrofoam
and little white squares flutter onto the ground behind her;
a boy in shorts, yellow t-shirt,
pushes a wooden cart,
"*Riddim*" painted on the sides in black, green and gold,
    Kisko-pop!
    Buy yu kisko-pop!
and Shirley Jean's slippers come
    clap clap on the pavement,
the straps unloose around her ankles
while across the street, Marse Wilbert
selling the daily news,
from under the betting shop piazza,
winks at Shirley, points to the headlines:
"Man Commits Suicide Over Pretty Woman",
styrofoam landing softly on his hair,
    Kisko-pop!
      Gleaner!
    Traffic moves slow,
someone in a new Volvo
    honks
at the "*Riddim*" cart boy
The tinted window slides down,
a white-sleeved arm signals for a *Gleaner*,
the bus behind – *Jah Man,* Number 35
    honks
at the Volvo,
Jah Man's riders stick their heads out;
Maggie holds up her cup,
    Gleaner!
the bus driver spits onto the road

and Shirley Jean crosses the street,
a basket of pomegranates balanced on her head;
    the Volvo honks,

Maggie knocks on the tinted windows,
the styrofoam cup already picked half-way down,
    the bus honks,
    Outta the way!

Maggie knocks on the tinted windows;
the driver spits and pomegranates tumble from Shirley's basket,
roll onto the road,
    the bus honks,
    honks;

Maggie knocks on the tinted windows,
the Volvo speeds away,
Jah Man's riders pull their heads in,
red seeds scatter.

THE LAYING OF HANDS

And then Reverend Berford stood up,
black cloaked, his arms spread,
the tips of his sleeves pointing too to the straight and narrow way,
his hands, two tablets of stone – *Glory!*
And the organist struck a note:
a wail that brought the deacons to their feet as
all at once a moan rose from the back pew,
moving down the aisles,
gathering strength over each bowed head
until in the front row the women flung their arms in the air – *Hallelulah!*
And there came Papa Sita's son, Ernest
(the one with nine fingers), weeping,
and the reverend, the deacons, and all the elders
laid white palms on his shoulders
and prayed in a voice that raised the wilted cassia on the windowsill – *Yes!*
and as the prayers rose higher through
the dusty beam of sunlight over Reverend Berford's head,
the hands pressed ever harder on Ernest's shoulders
as Exodus, Leviticus, Revelation and more
fluttered their thin-leaved wings to the chant of "*Thou shalt not*"
and all the while the deaconesses swayed together – *Holy!*
their dresses white like cotton used to wrap the dead.
Then with the gush of a door flung open,
Sister Gilda screeched like the trumpet of the seventh angel,
sending the prayer in Berford's throat to wedge between his teeth
as the candles flickered
and the picture of the last supper fell from the wall,
the people scattering like bleating goats,
Ernest left alone,
Christ peering through the window,
his pierced palms pressed against the stained glass.

WAITING FOR THE SECOND COMING

These days there's a stillness.
It's in the way the rain bird
stands and stares,
beak clamped shut over the day's pickings,
claws pressed in the soft clay.
Outgrowing its pot,

the croton on the windowsill leans,
yellow-red leaves press against the pane like fingers.
The neighbour's mongrel dog has a twitch on his mouth;

he lies on his stomach watching by the front gate;
and the preacher in town doesn't scream anymore.
Mouthing prayers,
he paces the corner at Harbour and King.
People walk past,

folded newspapers clutched under their arms;
they glance at the sky.
Through clouds, the sun's outlined with a golden wedding band,

and something's changed in the way evening comes:
the shadow of the lime tree lengthens way across the yard,
and at sunset, ants march into the crack in the kitchen wall.
Mrs. Hillary on Mimosa Avenue has stopped her fanning –
twenty years of rocking on the front porch,

and she hadn't missed a beat.
The rocker creaks,
flies hover the ripe tomato patch;
while nights,

behind white lace, the moon is bright and moist as a lover's eyes,
and even the crickets, conscious of their voices, *know*.

The watchers wait

as John Crows' wings,
      heavy as medieval robes,
sweep lower.
Red vulture eyes
          circling the tin roof tops,
closer   closer.

But oh, in the distance –
a small black cloud,
a promise the size of a man's fist.
Yes, verily, verily,
He will come to save them.
The watchers wait for such a time as this.

NIGHTFALL

In that moment   between light and dark,
something in the mind   whirls,

and what you see
        in your near death

are mules   everywhere
                        sprouting wings,
and in the window —
                a kerosene lamp,
Home Sweet Home
illuminated in letters
        on the glass shade.

HALF-MOON

LEAVING FOR OHIO

My father is humming, *At the cross, at the cross.*
In the dusk, the long hills lit up with veranda lights
encircle Kingston, a rhinestone bracelet
on the wrinkled arm of an old woman.
And except for the drunk asleep beneath a stinking-toe tree,
cradling his bottle of Red Stripe beer,
the roads to the Palisadoes are still empty.
Driving the old Ford van,
where I first saw the light,
my father taps his fingers on the steering wheel;
mother stares at a ship in the harbour,
the sea smooth like the skin across her shoulders.
Norman Manley Airport, five miles, and
there is something I must say before I go,
the burden of my heart,
something about my father, smiling,
meeting me after school, my first day at kindergarten,
his hair parted on the side,
white sleeves rolled up to the elbows.
Something about him driving across Bog Walk Bridge
    in the thick rain,
            the van with bad wipers:
we were so safe,
my mother waiting for us at home,
porcelain plates painted with blue roses,
a mound of white rice to the left of the roses.

At the airport, my father unloads the suitcase packed
with mother's black cake, fried fish wrapped in foil,
bun, a tin of Milo, a bottle of guava jelly,
a purple orchid between the pages of a volume of poems.
The suitcase leaves on a conveyor belt,
    disappears into a dark square;
my mother's eyes shine

like the wet glaze of the porcelain plates left on the dish rack;
and there is something I must say before I go.
When I was little we pressed our heads together
under the almond tree at Seaward Drive,
she brushing her lashes against mine.
My father holds me,
pats me on the back with the same strong hand
used to grasp his cutlass, chop sugarcane on the mountainside.
Last boarding call,
    and already the green hills are far away.

From the airplane window
they seem so small.
She is the woman on the waving gallery
wearing the black and blue dress with the white collar;
her fingers in the wire fencing
like a child watching from a yard across the street.
He is the man to her left, in the light coloured shirt,
his hand in his pocket, humming,
    the burden of my heart.

POSTCARDS

On my way to Cleveland.
Here's a lone tree in a field —
the leaves red as the beans we shelled afternoons on the back porch.

A solitary bird perched on a silo —
it reminded me of you waiting by the mailbox in your orange hat.

Weeping willows,
so many of them.

Fields... dry now,
beige and rough as stubble.

More weeping willows.

Barns bulky as coffins.
A row of birds — a family of eight huddled on a wire,
black robed, beaks frozen shut.

Evening now, the wires make shadows,
staves traced on the snow
(note — the birds are gone.)

This is silence:
white covering everything—
the fields, the roof tops, the moon.

(How are the water hyacinths
there against the whitewashed wall?)

Cows bury their heads in hay,
tails limp.
The barns are white mounds.

Here is a river,
frozen and glistening like a snake.
Crossing, I must be light as pollen.

Meet you in January
We will sip sorrel among the crotons
and watch the lizards change colour –
green, greener, greenest –
as the mailman comes up the gravel road on his yellow bicycle,
his bell ringing clear as a toast of crystal goblets,
his hand waving empty,
satchel flapping against his hip –
as he passes on through the avenue of trees.

LIVING ROOM PORTRAITS

I have rearranged the living room furniture.
The sofa faces south now,
so on clear days I can see my mother.
Through beige paint she is off-coloured,
but if I hold my head still, and focus,
I see her small white house there between two mango trees,
and out back, the broken chicken coop,
the stub of the otaheite tree,
and white towels spread on zinc, bleaching in the sun.
My mother stands in the front doorway,
one shoe off,
right foot rubbing against the ankle of the left.
Her eyes fit over mine –
perfect as the teaspoons stacked in her top kitchen drawer.
I am looking into the black dot in her eye,
through the back door
and I see myself, eleven years old, peeping
from behind a cocoa tree.
There is the smell of roasted corn and carbolic soap,
the hum of a foot-peddled sewing machine,
the swish of a machete in the bushes.
Now I watch myself play jacks on the kitchen floor,
drink the cup of condensed milk sprinkled with nutmeg
left for me on the counter,
linger awhile by the louver windows
where nylon curtains billow behind me,
puffed like the sails of an old schooner.
I trace red rivulets in mother's eyes.
Thin as the skin in broken eggs,
my lids close over hers,
as the moon in my throat bobs
and night tide pulls at my tongue,
warm and salty.

THE *ASCANIA* DOCKS IN SOUTHAMPTON, CIRCA 1955

All that's left now is a black and white photo from an old *Daily Mirror*
One thousand West Indian immigrants on board the *Ascania*—
mostly men in felt hats.
Flooding the decks, they lean over the rails,
their shoulders pressed together.
On the far left is someone's Uncle Morris.
He has left behind half an acre of yellow yam
and a girl with a pretty black mole on her upper lip.
The dream in his eyes shines like the lighted window far away,
where by candle light,
the girl washes her hair in a plastic basin.
Wearing new shoes and a relative's old wedding suit,
the young man behind him searches the dock for the Queen.
Certainly, she will come to greet him,
her gloved hand waving like the white wing of a dove.
Short men. Tall men. Husky men. Frail men.
Men with five pounds in their pockets
and a cardboard suitcase with a broken latch.

Come to the Mother Country
The Mother Country needs you.
The cry crossed the Atlantic,
ringing from Trinidad and Tobago
and along the curve of the Leewards,
past Anguilla and on to the Cockpit Country of Jamaica.
Brave men. They packed their bags,
their ancestors' fear of ships already strained from their blood,
the Atlantic spread before them like a banquet table.

Now on the upper deck, the fifth person from the right –
a man smiles, rubbing his chin.
Union Jacks are stuffed in the bags beneath his eyes.
Later, he will take a train to Victoria Station.
In the cold and the rain, there will be no one to meet him.

He will work in an asbestos plant,
rent a flat with a mattress
and a clothes line strung from one corner to the other.
He will dream of children playing on warm rocks by the Martha Brae,
their mothers bathing silently in the water.

JANUARY, BINGHAMTON NY

In this place
I don't know the names of birds
or the tree in the yard across the street
or what hills I see through my window
spread like welts across the cold back of the earth.
What stories do grandmothers tell here?
and what ancient memory drives the wind
to whimper and wail whimper and wail against the kitchen door?

Nights when icicles line the windowsills,
jagged like the teeth which rake me,
I would be sister to wind's call

(what a wailing
what a wailing
what a wailing
Lord,
what a wailing
what a wailing)

had it not been for those mornings,
      the snow
               blowing like confetti from a wedding basket,
                    onto the bird on the church steeple,
            into the arms of the tree in the neighbour's yard,
                        covering the forgiving hills,
the bowed heads of the grandmothers,
softly now
      hushhush
no need to whimper
           no need
no need to
wail.

NIGHT MOTHS

After you said goodbye last summer,

white moths came.
At first there were only three,
        brushing against the window
                wings thin as fresh tissue paper for swaddling
the flowers of the grieving.
        And such urgency –
                        wing to glass
                                wing to glasswing to glass
                                                wing –

What could be meant by a visitation of moths?

Later,   there were more –
dozens!
Without a sound,   they flew
        onto the ceiling
                        the arms of a rocking chair
    my comfy slippers
                    the soft folds of curtains.
For two weeks they stayed
    listened to the accordion player next door,
                watched Brentwood on t.v.
                            heard Mr Graff groan downstairs;
I touched one perched on a door frame –
            it fluttered its wings,

                                left my fingers
                    dusted with baby powder.

Suddenly, one Tuesday they died
white wings folded on the hard wood floor.
It was after more news from Rwanda:
a mad woman boarded up and abandoned

                                        one eye
watching from a hole in the wall.
She
had eaten
the hearts
of dead children
to stay
alive
                                        and how
she longed
to exchange
her heartpain
for mine
your goodbye   unnoticeable
as one
missed beat
in her chest –

                        white moths,

perching
at the corners of her mouth,
                on both dark eyelids

                and the widening space between her breasts.

LAMP REPAIRS

I

Ad in the yellow pages:
Lights Unlimited
Visit our showroom
Your one-stop lighting outlet
Over 700 lamps on display
Parts and expert lamp repairs.

II

We had a red light bulb strung from the back porch
and hung high in the otaheite tree in the back yard.
Nights, like lilies blushing beneath it,
we sat on the steps telling stories –
I told my cousin, Olivia,
the bulb was there for fruit to ripen red
and she believed me.

Summers, angels stretch their halos wide,
wear them like Hula-Hoops
and dance and dance
their waists shimmering white light.

A beautiful golden table rises from the Rio Cobre at noon,
many pursue it, all die gasping,
sucked in by current.
Some call the table an illusion:
sunlight playing on a copper bed.

III

In a gift shop in town,
twenty four night-lights
shaped like praying hands
line a wall –
translucent fingers cast in mold.
What if one night,
all the hands should unfold?

IV

If you lose your way,
light a candle,
look deep into the flame,
see the almond eyes of your priestess/warrior ancestors
pointing the way home.

Do not disturb the flies in your lamp shade,
they have drifted to sleep,
warm,

and at peace

drunk with light.

WILD RICE

I

Before she stole away,
Mama Pansa braided grains of rice into her hair;
tying it with a red cloth.
Later, in the dark hills safe from barking dogs,
she loosened her plaits,
seeds falling like soft rain
into the cupped palms of her children.

II

At the corner of Broad and High there is a wedding.
The grandmother of the bride wears cream chiffon;
she is raising a thin arm, her hand clutching the old rice
                                        swept up from her own wedding –
a flick of the wrist, and   sudden as memory

                        rice fills the air
one long grain   resting
on a high cheekbone.

III

Here is your coat of arms:
two and a half cups of rice
one cup of red beans
a dry coconut, a little garlic, a little thyme,
quarter teaspoon black pepper, a few pinches of salt.
No instructions needed.

IV

The crows in the back yard don't care
whether spilled rice is brown or white.
They perch on the edge of your roof, waiting
for more.

V

In Half-way-tree, a madwoman paces all day,
gently dropping grains of rice into an enamel basin.
The sound, pitter pat
over
pitter pat pat pat
and over,
reminds her of night rain on a zinc roof.
She is a rainmaker and on a day like today, hot and sticky with memory,
will rain out the Queen's parade
if she wants to.

VI
What makes rice wild?

VII

A child sits at the kitchen table picking out bad rice,
her mother singing old-time songs,
savouring them, slowly –
one line, *steal away*
then a long pause,
a little salt in the pot,
a light stir,
then another, *steal away*
    pause –

VIII

In this small zinc house,
we go to bed with bellies fluffed full of white rice
and we all know that the patter of the rain against our window
is really the swollen finger tips of the forgotten dead
longing
      to come in.

From New York to Arizona
you've been on this Greyhound bus for two and a half days
and now, long plateaus
are muted red tombstones of memories which do not belong to you
and will not take you back
to who you are.
Wasn't Gran'pa Cyril's small grey tomb
under the lime tree in the Elgin yard enough?
Death is the perfect moment for remembering–
                    (the rhythm of cane cutting,
            the eyes of hurricanes,
                                the rhythm of cane cutting,
        the eyes of hurricanes)
That's why the dead rest,
while the living are busy with imagi-

nation. *Gran'pa!*
If you could hear my imaginings,
I know you would laugh a belly laugh
so deep
that even the green limes them
would plu-pluup
    pluup
            pluup.
off the lime tree
and you would say in your ready tongue:
this is a true-true ting.

I'M AFRAID OF LOSING THINGS

like you eating sugar cane on the back steps,
                    singing by the hibiscus hedge,
   the freckles on your neck
as you fry johnny-cakes on the stove,
                   sit fanning on the verandah,
or stand on your small feet
       ironing on the back porch,
   laughing on the telephone,
wearing a sabbath dress
with your face shut tight in prayer,
   holding me at the airport,
       the wind on your floppy hat,
sun filling your eyes.
Now that your hair is gray
I remember you sitting in church
with your legs crossed at the ankles,
                  raking the leaves in the front yard,
     scolding the dog who left
paw prints on the floor,
             feeding the chickens,
   the moons on your finger nails.
And I'm afraid of losing you,
now that your hair is gray.

EN ROUTE

Leaving Kingston,
twelve thousand feet
and sand outlines the coast – gold

              dust swept along by a fine-tipped paintbrush.
Beside you, an old woman looks and sighs; she knows:
is not everyting that have sugar taste sweet.
Clouds come,
and you leaf through a magazine –
ads for   travel bags,
           travel clocks,
           travel pillows,
               sale priced cassettes of
The American Accent Program; while
the old woman, glasses resting on her bosom,
                  shifts in sleep and dreams
                        (Dos'el dear, not doe'sile)
and in her dream, horses are everywhere
                (You mean dos'el like a d-o-c-i-l-e horse right?)
     kicking up dust *(Say after me)* with their hooves
and clouding the *(dossdoss dossdoss)* window   sudden
    as the memory
of nutmeg sprinkled over a warm bowl of meal.

New York, twelve thousand feet
and the city appears below you,
               bright as a new gold tooth.
The cockpit dims;
(this will not be easy)
and you straighten your seat
as the old woman waking   breaks into tongues:
Oh shali-doss shali-rass shali-shali-shali-shali-seeee shali-shali-shali-shali-raaaas
Could it be safe there – all those bridges
              across the Hudson suspended by lights?

WATFORD MEMORIAL, LABOUR ROOM NO.4

I remember when I was born –
someone's fingers cold
and long like the slow rain trickling down the window,
held my head;
my mother sighed, *hhhhhhhn.*
I had heard that sound before
muffled by water running into the tub
as she kneeled and scrubbed kneeled and scrubbed
the ring around my father's collar,
hhhhhhhn.
September, it rustled against airmail to home—
paper blue and thin as English sky spread meager over the yard—
How things in Jamaica?
Three months, the baby almost due;
the ink dark against the blue page,
a little susumba would do my mouth good,
she sealed the letters: *Hhhhhhhn.*
October
November.
Mother hobbled, *hhhhhhn,* from the chair at the kitchen table,
scrubbed the grease from the pots,
the linoleum on the floor,
the fingerprints on the refrigerator, *hhhhhhn,*
kneeled and scrubbed kneeled and scrubbed the rings
                                    around my father's sleeves,
the rings
the rings
around his collar his collar his collar,
kneeled and scrubbed,
hhhhhhhn.

At the winter solstice, the sun far away
when I was *hhhhhhhn* born,
hhhhhhhn

53

born,
hhhhhhhn
born.
I gathered all my mother's groans,
squeezed them into my throat
and screamed.

EIGHT-POINTED STAR

VOICE LESSON FROM THE UNLEASHED WOMAN'S UNABRIDGED DICTIONARY

Cimarrón.
Cimarrón.
Remember to roll the r's.
(Think of the sound of galloping mustangs on a Nevada plain)
Cimarrón
(or the pound of buffalo hoofs)
Cimarrón
(or your grandma's mules broken loose last year.)

Maroon.
Maroon
Breathe in deep,
say it like a warrior hurling her spear through the air.
Maroon
(Now think of bloodhounds, armed men at your heels)
Maroon
(or Nanny's boiling cauldron set to catch them)
Maroon
(or women wearing the teeth of white soldiers around their ankles.)

Maroon.
Pronounce the "a" soft like the "a" in "alone."
That's right,
marooned.
(Imagine dangling from an orange tree, blindfolded –
stockings from someone's clothesline noosed around your neck)
Marooned.
(or the one dollar to your name,
the eviction notice taped to the door)
Marooned.
(think of a cold, soundproof room.)

Maroon.
Say it slow like a rich, full thing to the mouth –
Maroon
(Remember yourself, six years old, talking sassy
                                        in your mother's dark lipstick)
Maroon
(or Zora's lips mouthing *"just watch me,"*
                                her felt hat tilted to the side of her head)
Maroon
(or all those women's mouths in Ebenezer choir, *Free at Last,*
singing for the fire locked up in their bones.)

Here's your chance now,
follow the instinct of your tongue
and say it your way,
Maroon.
Put on that hat you wear when you're all stirred up and need to have a word or two.
Hurl your spear if you like,
or change the accent on the "a" –
perhaps something wide, free like the "a" in gallop –
Maroon!
(Hear the call of an old abeng?)
Maroon!
Say it
Say it rich
Say it full
(The twitch near your ear is only the remembrance of thunder.)
But listen.
Listen for the feet of summer rain behind you.
Say it strong
Say it *now*
Break loose speckled horse,
and take yourself back.

NANTUCOMPONG

(For Maroon Nanny who folded back her hands between her legs and
caught the shots of fifty soldiers, teaching us 'Nantucompong'.)

In streets along Kingston Harbour
down by river gullies
on yam hillsides
you see them –
their necks long
the ridge of their lips swollen and dangerous.
They can feed a house full of mouths
with a little saltfish, two handfuls of flour.
Rise up against them
and their eyes send you limping
back into the macca bush.
In skirt pockets and cotton pouches in brassieres
they have tea leaves
to check bad colds
heal up wounds
drive out thieving neighbours
send a grown man to the kitchen floor repentant on his knees
and even the mad dogs know
                              their shadow across the road
can drive out legions.
With bare hands, they'll steal hot coals
to warm a little milk for the children's tea;
stone them
curse them –
they catch words between their teeth
and spit them out – *tu!*
Kill them
and years later, there they are –
some girl, eyes on fire,
clutching her school bag on the subway in New York.

BLESSED HARVEST:
TO THE WOMAN IN THE PAINTING ON MY LIVING ROOM WALL

On a sales table in Columbus, Ohio,
I found you waiting,
the white slits of your eyes
watching from among Raphael's cherubs,
O'Keefe's petunias at your feet.

You had come from a long way –
all those years of picking apples in Arkansas,
to pay back the money your daddy owed Mr. Wilkins
for the debt his daddy owed Mr. Wilkin's daddy
for an acre of land and a horse that ran away with a brand new saddle.
All those years of birthing and burying:
Opal born dead, a blue cord around her throat;
Aston drowned in the Red River, New Years eve 1915;
Lily sucking her thumb, picking her hair – stopped breathing.

How many tiny feet warmed in the folds of your skirt?

You have arms long
enough to reach backwards and forwards in time.
Once, your fingers made shadows – sunflowers
      on the window
for a child crying in Soweto;
                and your elbow has rested on the shoulder
of Billie Holiday singing
the blue

      blue

blues;
you offered her pine nuts, wild berries
gathered along the Mississippi from Cairo, Illinois to New Orleans
where the backs of your wrists

stroked the cheek of great-grandmother, Millie,
crying, strapped to her mother on a ferry bound for Baton Rouge;
yes, you've known railroads covered with wild onion, dandelions and thyme,
have chopped through forest
                    waded through swamp
(brown mud-circles mark your thighs.)
Picking peaches in Georgia on Mr. Wilkin's grandson's land,
you heard Aston moan when MLK got shot,
held three long fingers to his forehead,
three long fingers to the lips of MLK.
Later, someone would remember
the smell of lemon grass and cloves.

The man at the cash register put you in a big black bag,
dark inside like the earth is to turnips and potatoes ready for reaping.
All the way on the bus, (what secrets lay under the pits of your arms?)
I hear you breathing, whispering to get out:

> *Blessed Harvest*
> *Blessed Harvest*

Down Morse Road, around the corner at Maize,

> *Blessed Harvest*

Down Cleveland, across Hudson,

> *Blessed Harvest*
> *Blessed Harvest*
> *Blessed Harvest*

Left on High, 9th Avenue to Neil,
           the ends of your scarf blowing from the top of the bag,

> *Blessed Harvest.*

Leaning on my living room wall,
your arms your arms your arms,
stretch
offering a basket of plenty:
corn, carrots, *blessed* turnips, green peppers,
potatoes, apples,   *BlessedBlessedBlessedBlessed*
hallelujah,

      Harvest.

EXCERPT FROM THE BLOATED WOMAN'S
BOOK OF HUNGER

Madda Winnie dressed up in garbage bags
at Half-Way-Tree
has not eaten for days.
   Hunger for revolution has bored a hole
         through her navel
  and bloated her stomach;
      her eyes
shift back
       and forth,
this way
        and that way,
watching the earth
          as it whirls
    on its axis
in a frenzied dance
        around frenzied light.
Tilting her head
  at that precise angle which prevents dizziness,
she beckons to school children,

whispering: *Come, look. Listen to me, nuh?*
The children stop;
jump a little ring-a-ding,
then run, laughing.

Perhaps, she could wait instead
for the tiny feet
of the unborn,
but they will arrive
late and even further removed,
    from the centre
       of passing memory.

So tonight,
         a wheel in the middle of a wheel,
her bloated belly

                    will explode

                                   into necessary words –
circling   and separating
         into half-moons   and blazing lights
                                   enough to stir the bones
of the long-dead
                    whose dark marrow

                                   seeps deep
into the hidden core of the earth.

In the meantime,
                    there is evidence of disturbed blood:
the twitch of a lip, an eyelid, an ear,
                         and always

                                   coconut trees   leaning
closer to the ground.

THE GIFT OF TONGUES

When Daddy got baptised in Yallahs River,
he rose up speaking –
Oh-shali-waa-shali-mahi-wa.
His eyes shut tight as a newborn's,
someone wrapped him in a white sheet
and led him out of the water.
The brethren clapping and singing redemption,
the white-wings flew
Mahi-shali-ma
from tree to tree along the winding bank.
Daddy would never be the same –
he was filled,
the tongues always waiting to erupt from his lips,
Oh-shali-waa-shali-mahi-wa.
Week after week, he had knelt at the altar,
his mouth open,
waiting to be anointed Child of God.
Now, at Wednesday night prayer meetings,
Daddy flung up his arms
Oh-shali-waa
in the air
his feet keeping time on the red tile floor.
Surely, he had the gift of tongues;
Daddy wouldn't pretend,
would he?

Years have passed now, and I understand:
Daddy spoke for the feeling, not just the language.
It's like after a woman's been in labour for days,
and then a small body is pushed from between her legs,
Oh, shali.

Or like after you've trekked Blue Mountain peak,
so far
so far
so far
and you reach it,
but there are no words to say,
Shali mahi wa.

I picture myself an old woman on a sofa.
Blue light slants through the blinds
and makes horizontal marks like notepaper on the wall.
I fill in the lines:
Oh shali waa,
shali mahi wa.
Shali.
Shali.

OTHER RECENT POETRY TITLES FROM PEEPAL TREE

BETWEEN THE FENCE AND THE FOREST
JENNIFER RAHIM

Comparing herself to a douen, a mythical being from the Trinidadian forests whose head and feet face in different directions, Jennifer Rahim's poems explore states of uncertainty both as sources of discomfort and of creative possibility. The poems explore a Trinidad finely balanced between the forces of rapid urbanisation and the constantly encroaching green chaos of tropical bush, whose people, as the descendants of slaves and indentured labourers, are acutely resistant to any threat to clip their wings and fence them in, whose turbulence regularly threatens a fragile social order. In her own life, Rahim explores the contrary urges to a neat security and to an unfettered sense of freedom and her attraction to the forest 'where tallness is not the neighbour's fences/ and bigness is not the swollen houses/ that swallow us all'. It is, though, a place where the bushplanter 'seeing me grow branches/ draws out his cutting steel and slashes my feet/ since girls can never become trees'.

Jennifer Rahim was born and grew up in Trinidad. Her first collection of poems, *Mothers Are Not the Only Linguists* was published in 1992. She also writes short fiction and criticism. She currently lectures in English at the University of West Indies in Jamaica.

SPECIFICATIONS
ISBN: 1-900715-27-9
Price: Stg£7.99 / US$13.60 / CAN$19.20
Pages: 88
Date of Publication: July 2002

HORIZONS
STANLEY GREAVES

Stanley Greaves brings a painter's perceptions and musician's ear to the writing of this substantial selection of his poetry written over the past forty years. He describes his painting as 'a kind of allegorical story-telling' and the same kind of connections between the concrete and the metaphysical are found in his poems.

Greaves guesses at a background that includes African, Amerindian and European ancestry, but declines to relate to any of these in an exclusive way. Rather he writes out of a creole sensibility that celebrates Guyanese diversity: Afro-Guyanese folkways, Amerindian legend and Hindu philosophy.

To enter the collection is to discover a whole, self-created world of Blakean richness, one which is never static, but growing to encompass new elements. Greaves' is a dialectical vision, alert both to the movements of history and the minutiae of daily change.

Stanley Greaves was born in Guyana. He studied art in the UK and was head of the Division of Creative Arts at the University of Guyana for several years. He left Guyana in the 1980s and has been resident in Barbados since that time. He is one of the Caribbean's most distin-guished artists with major exhibitions in the UK (The Elders, with Brother Everald Brown) and Europe as well as throughout the Carib-bean. The collection includes ten line drawings by Stanley Greaves.

SPECIFICATIONS
ISBN: 1-900715-57-0
Price: Stg£9.99 / US$17.00 / CAN$24.00
Pages: 162
Date of Publication: July 2002

MICHAEL GILKES
JOANSTOWN AND OTHER POEMS

Between the long title poem and the other poems in the collection, Michael Gilkes sets up a dialogue about the nature of memory and the meaning of experience across time. 'Joanstown' is the recreation, in the voice of a younger self, speaking with all the intensity of first love, of the interweaving of person and place (the more elegant gracious Georgetown of the 1940s, with its 'cross-stitching of avenues, bridges, canals), and of a marriage whose seeming perfection leads to hubris.

The very concreteness of the recreation of a time when happiness came so easily is made the more moving for the reader by the framing awareness of its evanescence.

The other poems in the collection, in the voice of maturity, with all the consciousness of loss as a constant of life, explore the nature of memory as consolation.

Michael Gilkes is a noted Caribbean literary critic, dramatist (*Couvade*) film-maker and pioneer of multi-media presentations. He is Guyanese by origin, taught for many years at UWI, Barbados and has recently been living in Bermuda.

SPECIFICATIONS
ISBN: 1-900715-76-7
Price: Stg£7.99 / US$13.60 / CAN$19.20
Pages: 72
Date of Publication: July 2002

RALPH THOMPSON
VIEW FROM MOUNT DIABLO

A novel in verse, *View from Mount Diablo* explores the transformation of Jamaica from a sleepy colonial society to a postcolonial nation where political corruption, armed gangs, drug wars, and an avenging police and army have made life hell. Class and racial privilege and the resentments they provoke underscore both the turmoil in the wider society and the relationships at the heart of the narrative between Adam Cole, the dreamy white Jamaican boy who becomes a crusading journalist exposing the hidden godfathers of crime, squint-eyed Nellie Simpson, once the servant who cares for/abuses him, who becomes a political enforcer, and stuttering Nathan the gardener and groom, whose boyhood love for Adam is tested to the full when Adam's journalism threatens to expose his role as a cocaine baron. Beyond this trio is a dazzling array of real and fictive characters including Bustamente, Tony Blake aka 'The Frog', Blaka, an informer who finds religion, a white plantation owner still trying to wield power, and a suicidal police officer.

Louis Simpson, the Jamaican-American Pulitzer Prize-winning poet writes: '*View from Mount Diablo* is a remarkable achievement. Its knowledge of the island, the entwining of private lives and politics, lifts Jamaican poetry to a level that has not been attempted before. The poetry is strong, imaginative, fascinating in detail. It describes terrible things with understatement, yet with compassion. I don't think anything could be more harrowing than the rape of Chantal, or the boy begging Alexander to spare his life... This is narrative poetry at its best. Not only Jamaicans, but I think readers in England and the USA, will appreciate this book. It is something new.'

SPECIFICATIONS
ISBN: 1-900715-81-3
Price: Stg£7.99 / US$13.60 / CAN$19.20
Pages: 64
Date of Publication: December 2002

—

Peepal Tree Press publishes a wide selection of outstanding fiction, poetry, drama, history and literary criticism with a focus on the Caribbean, Africa, the South Asian diaspora and Black life in Britain. Peepal Tree is now the largest independent publisher of Caribbean writing in the world. All our books are high quality original paperbacks designed to stand the test of time and repeated readings.

All Peepal Tree books should be available through your local bookseller, though you are even more welcome to buy books direct from our online store at www.peepaltreepress.com. You can, of course still order by mail or phone. When ordering a book direct from us, simply tell us the title, author, quantity and the address to which the book should be mailed. Please enclose a cheque or money order for the cover price of the book, plus £1 / US$3.20 / CAN$5.50 towards postage and packing.

Peepal Tree sends out regular e-mail information about new books and special offers. We also produce a yearly catalogue which gives current prices in sterling, US and Canadian dollars and full details of all our books. Contact us to join our mailing list.

You can contact Peepal Tree at:

17 King's Avenue
Leeds LS6 1QS
United Kingdom

e-mail hannah@peepaltreepress.com
tel: 44 (0)113 245 1703

website: www.peepaltreepress.com